TOUGH

Published 2005
by

STACK
BOOKS

Smokestack Books
PO Box 408, Middlesbrough TS5 6WA
Tel : 01642 813997
e-mail : info@smokestack-books.co.uk
www.smokestack-books.co.uk

Cover design and print by
James Cianciaruso
j.cianciaruso@ntlworld.com

Author photograph by A.M. Reinink

ISBN 0-9548691-5-X

Smokestack Books
gratefully acknowledges the support of
Middlesbrough Borough Council
and Arts Council North East.

Smokestack Books is a member of
Independent Northern Publishers
www.northernpublishers.co.uk

Acknowledgements

Versions of some of these poems were first published in *The Flesh of the Bear, Sand, Sentinel, Smelter* and *Write Around*. An earlier version of 'Ride the Red Dragon' appeared in The Wrong California – Middlesbrough Laureate Poems (Mudfog 2004).

'I See You Seeing Me' was developed as part of a collaboration with installation artist Naoyo Yamamoto in Visions Gallery, Ginza Tokyo in 1993. Prelude to The Twocca Crow King was developed as a part of a larger piece at the Hydrogen Jukebox with musicians Kevin Howard, Milo Thelwall and Shaun Lennox.

Thanks to: Andy Croft for showing the way, Bob Beagrie for inspiration, enthusiasm and feedback, Kev Cadwallander for powerful encouragement, Dougie Pincott, Karl Thompson and Kate Fox for the opportunity to first develop material on a live stage and to Jo Colley for participating in the live adventures that put many of these poems into their final form. Thanks finally to Rebecca for constant support and true faith.

TOUGH

Andy Willoughby

For Holly and for hope.

Contents

Walk Through the Whale Bone Archway

That's no longer there,
Is only a trace of memory
For most of us round here -

Whispered about
By the old folk
Late at night in care homes,

Who claim its influence
Can still be felt
When you walk lucky

Through the spot
Where it stood
Like a Star Trek prop

Spiralling wormhole
In time's continuum
You may tumble through:

Be catapulted back
To when the hill farmer's
Second son came home

From his Whitby days
With the bones
As his statement

On primo genitor
With the arctic chill
Lodged in him.

Or you may see
The men of iron
Carrying a broken body down

From the cathedral
Caverns underground
That swallowed hundreds:

Small time Jonahs
Who paid in blood
For the blue stone

That spans the world
In railway tracks
Of forgotten origin;

Almost as invisible
As these legendary jaws
We've travelled through.

I Was a Teenage Frankenstein

I was a teenage Frankenstein
Invented a body that wasn't mine -
Swollen in strange places at very dodgy times,
It rebelled against my faith and it set me up for crime
I chased it into shadows to re-communicate,
It ripped the head off my young love
And taught me how to hate.

I was a teenage Frankenstein
Installed a brain that wasn't mine -
It put words in my mouth filled me up with bile,
Wrote weird poems in secret files,
I chased it through the cities to teach it how to care,
It hid in public libraries
Reading books I wouldn't dare.

I was a teenage Frankenstein
Connected a heart that wasn't mine –
It beat a ragged rhythm and disrupted my rhymes
Emptied of blood and full of slime,
I chased it overseas to drain out all the hate
But it dragged me to Alaska
where we refrigerate.

I was a teenage Frankenstein
Until I admitted: this monster's mine.

For My Patron

Billy Razorblades comes to me from a global perspective
With his Clark Kent look and his monetarist invective,
He's power-dressed and pressed to make the right impression,
This superman makes dollars in the midst of a depression.
He "grabs them by the goolies" and keeps it "lean and mean",
He thinks a poem or two could keep the punters keen,
Of course he understands I create at my volition,
But Billy's commission comes with certain conditions:
Can I downsize my sonnet from fourteen lines to ten?
Cut out the vicious couplet that ends it with a sting?
Don't satirize or castigate the happy paying throng,
If they can't consume it mindlessly I'm doing something wrong.
Can I streamline my iambics from five strong beats to four?
It's good economics to keep them wanting more.
As for the content can I please keep it upbeat?
No ear-chopping angst for "the man on the street",
He may like my bad language but there I'm out of luck-
You can't flog it on the radio if you let slip a fuck!
Here's to Billy Razorblades he's cut me into shape,
With a moveable product endorsed by the state,
Who won't interfere but it's best not to alienate,
While we dump our caring products that are looking out of date,
I used to hate salesmen more than picket beating pigs,
Now with a bit more standardizing I'll get oil company gigs,
I'll formulate a double take on the pipelines strewn with flowers,
Sugar up the bitter fruit whilst the population cowers,
As governments top the dissidents I'll cover it with verse,
Cos Razorblades tells me unemployment is much worse,
Thanks to William I'm a twenty-first century man,

Writing for a living on the Coca-Cola can,
Writing for a living on the Coca-Cola can.

I See You Seeing Me

It rises within me:

Everything is changed
In the most domestic of moments

When you look at me these days
You see the golden surface
And you smile benignly

When I look at you
I catch the shadows
In the folds of the years
Taste the salt there
From the sweat of working hours

What's between us
Has been a long time
In the making

Like any seascape
Like any desert.

The Cold Steel

We were surprised by the man-made beauty
Of the Satsuma-coloured steelworks-sky
The night we were caught in the blackout.

When the darkness broke out suddenly around the rec,
We doorway huddled, desperate for some warmth,
Our eyes adjusting as the rippling beats of orange,

Emanating from the hell-mouth of the furnace,
Cast everything new in flickering shadows –
I swear I saw flames dance in your eyes!

Walking the same walk warm with whiskey.
Street lamps throw different shades,
Coaxing contemplation of my unfamiliar hands.

For a moment you're back there beside me;
Though the thrill of this ghostly communion
Vanishes into vacuums, as I stare at hard starlight

Winking through a sky of squid's ink black:
In this world where the steel's stopped flowing
All is hard and separate and infinity is cold.

Ride the Red Dragon
(for Dad and for the Boro)

(i)

128 years up
    in fireworks
      red flags waving
for Teesside pride
    we are red dragon riding
        in the land of Brains and bards
    high as the bubble that for once
      hasn't burst.
Getting our gobs around the strange word:
      winners.

(ii)

Ultramarine is my favourite colour,
Also known as Yves Klein blue,
Induces an electric vibe of calm,
When my mind is boiling crimson -

and red is the colour of my team

The fields in Kent where I learned,
The endless shades of combined words,
Were green as my springtime love:
I longed for cooling tower silhouettes!

and red was the colour of my team

The packages from home were brown,
Crackling with anticipation of results,
Mam sent every kick from our dirty old town,
Desperate for news that we could survive,

and red was the colour of my team

Royal blue swathed the iron lady
As the shipyards swiftly closed,
Chimneys and furnaces crashing down,
The queues grew longer for signing on,

and red was the colour of my team

The doom toll print was black,
Announcing the Boro's demise,
Grey padlock on Ayresome gates
Like a skinhead kick in the guts,

and red was the colour of my team

Multi-coloured newspapers arrived,
Pronounced tacky by the chattering class.
The scarlet shirts were my phoenix,
I have always read the paper backwards,

and red was the colour of my team

The whiskey glass was yellow gold,
In late night bedsits after waiting shifts,
To ill-mannered gents in penguin suits,
Who believe work's a matter of the will,

and red was the colour of my team,

In Japan the rice was purest white,
On Tatami floors I dreamed of home,
The papers kept arriving monthly,
Reminding me of who I'd been,

and red was the colour of my team

The towers of Wembley were white,
With dad breathing hard with angina,
As his childhood dreams dissolved,
For the third time in cockney blue,

and red was the colour of my team

The surgeon's knife shone silver,
That restored him for this final day,
Where a century of battered pride,
Rides the red dragon and flies away,

and red is the colour of my team.

(iii)

The stadium roof is closed at Cardiff,
We are Romans at the Coliseum,
Doing battle by proxy with history
That has traditionally struck us dumb,

With a century and a half of toil,
In industry that cripples and kills,
To raise family to face the tale
Of dormant furnaces and empty hills,

So our singing has a desperate joy
As it strains the metal ceiling,
Our ghosts rise up from within
In the final whistle's flood of feeling,

Not "only football" this hard won identity,
This generations-spanning mind-flash,
Of public memory and personal past,
These many thousand exhaled 'At last's

We'll win nowt and we'll take the pain,
With grim wit and some graveyard craic,
When the Boro let us down again,
Was the mantra of all our Grandparents,

All changed now as we take the silverware,
In a kaleidoscope of memory through tears,
Wilfy, Robbo, Big John and dead relatives
Flash before us as a second fills with years,

My Father and Uncle both speak to their Dad
"We did it at last – won in our lifetime!"
Generations of ghosts ride the red dragon
Through the roof and into this rhyme,

It's not just a game but life's very fabric:
Though this town deserves respect never given
For the steel structures that girdle the globe,
We'll take this cup as our symbol of hope.

Invaders

We were the stone killers of stranded suns,
My squealing sister and her friend recoiled
From our acts of pointless boy violence.
We ran from star beast to star beast,
Plopping bricks into the slick quivering
Of translucent crimson flesh.
These rocky shelves of petrified forest
Weren't revealed in childhood days,
But the Redcar sand with its oily flecks
Threw up their treasures and grotesques,
A hermit crab's big claw dangles
From the past of a white winkle shell,
Pointing to the multiple barefoot terror
Of the lion-maned plague of stinging red
That sudden scarlet Sunday morning.
A thousand jelly fish gleaming bright,
Every stellar heart stopped with a plop
As we embarked on a biblical slaughter;
Our eyes wide and blank in our purpose
Ears deaf to the girl's horror cries –
Island defenders defying the North Sea's roar,
Calling for her awful misborn.

Docking '91

(i)

Walking towards those
same metal monsters
that stretched
and broke my childhood's
distant skyline
I almost hear
a voice in the
dockside wasteland
where the eerie orange glow
from the molten
steel heating up
the coast mingles
and suffuses with
the moons cold blue
until existence
shifts from its round
of circular contractions
and lies flat
in a new colour scheme,
flat, except for the cranes.

(ii)

That big one's
the centre of
the universe.

That big one's
my early
memory.

That big one's
got a mind
of it's own.

My Granddad told me
he should know:
he drove it.

(iii)

He's gone now: he was such a huge man,
It seemed to me in younger years,
But he shrank and turned silent
When he saw something bigger drawing near.

In a way I'm glad he's gone,
At least he missed this bitter end-
The yards deserted the cranes creaking,
Old friend to rusty friend.

His crane's dinosaur head is poking sharp
At the oil slicked sea through the frozen dark,
Waiting for one last ship to come sailing in,
For one last crew to disembark.

Boot Hill

Grandad Fred and me shared a passion for cowboys,
Rode the plains of yesteryear with the masked man,
Laughed at Abbot and Costello on Saturday TV.
In the summer holiday chalet park in East Anglia
We'd solemnly visit the "grave of Billy the Kid" –
Boot Hill simulacra, where crosses stood impressive,
Epitaphs for Jesse James, Wyatt Earp and young Bonney.
The old man span a good yarn with his tonsured head,
Romantic propensity and hard-earned beer-belly,
Liked to show off his yellow crushed nicotine thumb:
Product of a crane cabin accident with grinding gears,
"It's not my gunhand though son" he would wisecrack,
Cocking back his other thumb to send me scurrying for cover.
Back-home bedroom wall's adorned with Billy's wanted poster,
Buckshee with Belle Starr's, from a tabloid mail-order give-away.
The bowler-hatted, squinty-eyed, young psychopath,
Stares out - head tipped back, rifle propped to hand,
Serial killer role model in a pose of deadly cool.
Truth is though, it wasn't the left-handed gun but Little Lou
Both Grandad and me were nearer to –
He talked a good fight the baccy rolling Teesside romancer,
But knew when to turn tail and leggit when the gobshite was done.
Me, I could make noises just like Costello,
With my amazing asthmatic squeezebox lungs,
With the "buh-buh-buh behind you Abbot!" look of horror.
In the glass now I find my own hair thinning and suck in my belly,
Gasp open mouthed like a fool for a moment,
Searching the mirror reflected hall shadows,
Sensing the kid lurking with well oiled Winchester,
Ready to be suddenly shoulder swung.
Decide to teach my daughter "who's on first?"
While I still remember the words.

Beamed Up

(for Nana)

Your clock was wrong for twenty years but you never replaced it.
You've stopped now too, like the old song never to go again, your
time all wrong at the end - not knowing the day or the hour, who
visited you, reminded every ten minutes, facts promptly forgotten,
ticker not tocking properly, blood in the brain too slow. Your old
black piano out of tune and un-played, gathering dust. Going out
of time, morphine confusion of lung cancer shadows, your strange
pronouncements, ambiguous in their nonsense and mythic response,
our books of Greek legends all infested with paper lice, your mother
forgot to dip your memory in the black river waters, you told me I
was a bloody fool on that death bed, it's true but I don't know why
you said it: my cap and bells invisibly jangling as I walk away from
the familiar Merlin Road door the day of your funeral, away from
the nicotine stained curtains and yellow plastic daffodils dustily
brightening up the Boyd's Estate sitting room for forty years, away
from the ghostly laughs of aunts, uncles, sisters, cousins, from the
Star Trek signature tune on the old brown T.V. you and I watched so
avidly. Away from the echo of my own child-voice in it's uncaged
imaginings. The last thing you said to me was "What else is there?"
in a seemingly lucid moment but it was hospital dinner-time and
whether you were calling for dessert or contemplating the end of
breathing I'll never be sure – "daft bugger", you laugh in your
eternal cloud of Embassy smoke. Eternity or custard? – as good an
epitaph as any.

Foreigner Policy

Love me: love my bomb!
It's got pictures of Macdonalds on,
Eat the burger! Eat the bun!
Collect the space wars plastic gun!
Love me: love my bomb!

Love it cos it's right,
It never will be left,
Love it cos it leaves the troublesome bereft,
Love it cos it's first world, top of the pile,
It can teach the dispossessed to bear it and smile,

Love me: love my bomb!
It's got pictures of John Wayne on,
Making money down the barrel of a gun,
Keeps the economy at number one,
Love me: love my bomb!

Love it cos it's smart-
It can ride a hoss!
Love it cos it knows
How to hit a little cross,
Love it cos it's clever in its high tech head;
Sometimes the cross is white sometimes it's red.

Love me: love my bomb!
It's got pictures of Bunny Girls on,
It can sing a freedom song,
Loves its country right or wrong
Love me:love my bomb!

Love it cos it's long,
Shiny and smooth,
Love it cos it pays,
It makes stock markets move,
Love it cos it costs taxpayers dollars-
It can employ a hundred thousand white collars.

Love me: love my bomb!
It's got pictures of Captain Kirk on,
It's got the power of exploding suns,
It never, never, never sets its phasers on stun,
Love me: love my bomb!

LOVE IT! LOVE IT! LOVE IT!
BLAM! BLAM! BLAM!

Love it cos it's big,
It can make a massive bang,
Of a no good rotten terrorist gang,
Stops 'em killing women for dressing up rude,
Or is it cos they're sitting on the price of crude?

Love me: love my bomb!
It's got pictures of Mickey Mouse on,
It can whistle a happy tune,
As it smashes through your kids bedroom
Love me, love my bomb!

"WAR! WHAT IS IT GOOD FOR?"
OIL COMPANIES!
VIRTUAL REALITY GAMERS!
SADISTIC JAILERS!
RECONSTRUCTION CONTRACTS!

ELECTION THROUGH FEAR!
OIL CONTRACTS!
MASS DISTRACTION!
LAST POST BUGLERS!
COFFIN MAKERS!
UNDERTAKERS!
PROSTHETIC LIMB MANUFACTURERS!
"HUH!"

"O say, can you see by the dawns early light…"

Provence

Today I am tired
Of badly dressed people
Who make luckless sprawling children
That they neglect and make stupid,
Screaming at them in supermarkets
In four letter words before
They hit them to make them good,
Never answering their curious questions
Till they ask them to themselves
In plaintive voices then don't answer,
Then stop asking and just make noise
Until they are smacked and scream.
I should write a social poem
Showing the system for what it is:
Reducing so many to ignorance
And poverty, and ignorance
Of their poverty,
And how keeping them stupid
Is a necessary pre-condition
For an elitist hierarchy.
But today I can't hack it
Lenin style,
I allow myself instead
The defeatist luxury of
Hating them all in their
Cheap tracksuits,
Rotten trainers and crap caps
Soggy hair and love bites,
Too big ear-rings and daft tattoos
And their poor squawking
Hopeless fucking brats.

I sing tunelessly along
To Abba's *The Winner*
Takes it All piped
Soullessly around
The well-stacked shelves,
Buy porridge that can
Be cooked in less
Than three minutes,
Olives imported
From sunny Provence.

X - Factor Girl

Look for the window with the ultra violet glow,
Blue light warning so the neighbours will know -
She's preparing her body for the local disco,

She looks like an orange,
But she's gonna get her man -
Cos she's the girl with the artificial tan

Thighs strain at her tight white skirt,
Stilettos are deadly as her perm starts to flirt,
She's looking for a man in a winter T-shirt -

She looks like an orange,
But she's gonna get her man,
Cos she's the girl with the artificial tan

Wants a real man doesn't want a mouse,
Wants a brain dead dickhead built like a house;
Arms like iron, chest like a horse -
Eats steak and eggs, hates "poufs" - of course,

She looks like an orange,
But she's gonna get her man -
Cos she's the girl with the artificial tan

Half past two and she's too drunk too know,
The faulty physique of the bloke she's got in tow,
He's a half-assed hippy, well gone on blow -

She looks like an orange
But she' s gonna get her man
Cos she's the girl with the artificial tan
Yeah she's the girl with the artificial tan.

The Ballad of Big Peter

The clumsy kid of little words,
Broke my best Robin Hood sword -

BIG PETER

Drove my sledge
Through the old school hedge -

BIG PETER

Snapped the trigger off my pop gun,
Lit fires when I told him to for fun-

BIG PETER

Necked the crow that we rescued,
When its wing just wouldn't glue -

BIG PETER

Was knuckle fisted and ham handed,
Dented the ground when he landed -

BIG PETER

Collected insects knives and sticks,
Drank Lowcock's pop till he was sick -

BIG PETER

Grew bigger than the dad who went away,
Practised on the punch-bag every day -

BIG PETER

Helped my old man wash his car,
When I stayed in to play guitar -

BIG PETER

Didn't read books like me,
nicked the apples from the trees -

BIG PETER

Went to Borstal at thirteen,
Said inside it was a scream -

BIG PETER

Gave me my first toke on a spliff,
Taught me that Deep Purple riff -

BIG PETER

Saved his best grin for me Mam,
Pushed me sister in her pram -

BIG PETER

Got a rep for seeing red,
Just one punch'll knock you dead -

BIG PETER

Showed me a gun under the floor,
Didn't ask what it was for -

BIG PETER

Kept himself free most of the time,
On the edge of violent crime -

BIG PETER

Packed in robbing took up Shylocking,
Kicks in doors now without knocking,
I hope you like this little poem,
Cos I'll tell you summat I still know him -

BIG FUCKING PETER!

Gaps

She smoked cigarettes four at a time,
The first time I really knew I'd seen her.
In the playground she played football with the boys,
Fought and swore but could be quiet as a murmur.

In the days before sunlight could be
Transformed into some idea of freedom,
We walked together saying nothing or joking;
When one of the horses in the fields off the estate

Broke free, she cried for it being run over:
The nervous, kicking, quick, black hoofing
Left us as wordless as the endless stream
Of numbness that soaked us to the bone,

With feelings unspoken with words redundant
On a red brick estate where our fathers
Drank themselves silent on Friday nights.
Or exhausted from work demanded silence:

"I've nowt to do with culture
so let me watch the snooker."
That desperate need for order
In a world of work and food and family.

She had given up her smoking the last time that I saw her.
We both had words we never knew when we first met,
But despite the clever way we filled the gaps,
There was more in the silences that we left.

Pre-match Prehistory

Captain Caveman in the Tube's bustling foyer,
Coming on all Neanderthal with the ticket machine;
The usual obscenities tumbling from drunken lips,
Headbutts hammering into the Perspex screen.

Big Ed, the mental nurse, knows the danger of empathy,
Motions "Mad" Gaz and me to do a Dionne Warwick-
Walk on by - though the ranting man's accent is our own,
Cut our cracking banter so passers-by know Trog is all alone.

Later we will impersonate this caveman in our colours,
With beery bitterness of defeat or condescending pride:
We have the savvy to handle match days in this Metropolis,
Won't let them see us as they label us – even on the piss.

Archaeology

Beneath the city, the card blurb tells me,
There lies remains of other lives and buildings
Glass cases offer me their concrete proof –
Prayer books, silver coins, dog skull truth.

In my fevered mind's eye grave worms wriggle
Timeless, I hear distant disembodied voices,
Refuse to fall into History's "great man" traps
Listen instead to those who refused to doff their caps!

Clink of utensils, clang of goblets,
Legends of beer, disease and bread:
Vague snatches of wild hopes for children
Marries my working life to the working dead.

Outside in the rain ears are battered timid,
Rhythmic rise and fall, big steam-hammer blast,
In the nearby prefab tired men bend over steaming tea,
Open-mouthed, silent, ears deaf to the distant past;

Dumb ancestors rot forgotten in illiterate graves.

Extra Ordinary

In pre–hypermarket days
The trek to Eston shops,
With Mam in flat shoes,
Tuesday and Thursday mornings.
Seeing her forearm muscles
Taut and tight,
Hands reddened
With two angry lines
From bulging bags
Of white plastic,
Me precociously impressed
By the younger mothers
Clip clopping
In white stilettos,
Bags swinging
Across long winter shadows,
Clinging to some
Film Noir idea of glamour -
Showing them my ability
To wire walk on the edge
Of The Magnet's red brick wall,
Where a few out-of-work men
Were steadily supping
Towards uneasy
Teatime sleep.

Out of Work with Crows

What of being out of work?
What do you remember of that?
I mean the crap jobs come easy -
Smell of mops, suds and pizza,
Fools who talked rubbish incessantly,
Hands red from sanded swarfega,
Counting the stolen hours and wages;
But what of the discarded months
Writing anxious letters,
Listing qualifications for strangers
Behind cold anonymous desks?
I remember one day counting the crows,
Ascending in hot air draughts from chimneys
Above the pine trees in the gardens
Of the next streets identical houses:
Graceful, hope-free, timeless.
There were seven in all,
Black and tireless ragamuffins in the moment,
Air thieves dancing –
You know I longed to be among them,
Floating feckless,
Free of application forms and measured language,
Rolling it all up into one glorious CAW!

Orpheus in His Cups

Make your own beautiful music,
Out of your humdrum pigging lives!
This is to set the record straight,
Sort out truth from jangling bardic lies,
I never turned back and looked 'er in the face,
A new idea for me music's what left her in that place -
Well you can't hang about when inspiration comes,
Not when it's good enough to strike the poets dumb,
Anyway, you don't think Hades that old necrophile-
Gives out real second chances down the darkest mile?
It weren't curiosity killed the cat but art's ambition,
The blind bastard couldn't sugar that with erudition.
Long before I lost her deep underground in t' dark
For playing wrong stuff from the wrong bit of me 'eart,
She told me straight she'd 'ad enough of composition,
That never delivered the ideal world but put her in collision,
With the things she dreamt of but could never become –
Like a cripple persuaded she could run,

"You and your fuckin' music!
Your beautiful fuckin' music!
It's only a bunch of useless notes,
Promising everything and giving nothing,
But the bitter fruit of dying hope"

Nothing you can see, I said in stuck up self-belief,
Nothing I can touch, she said and smacked me in the teeth.

Ah thought it was the right thing to do you surely see?
To use me gift to sing of mankind's atrocity,
Love songs shimmer but the stuff I'd 'ad in my face

Left me with the need to purge the foul dis-grace;
Homer was a fortunate fucker being dark struck:
To see in such times as we 'ad was the real bad luck.
He didn't see Achille's raging grief,
Or Patroclus anointed; still beautiful but rotten,
And then Hector's mangled corpse I've not forgotten:
All bloodied up and covered in horseshit and dead leaf.
That stuff though is the very least of it all,
Famous deaths always are next to those who fall unseen
By a world quick with monument and eulogy –
A player who can calm the sea gets to places you wouldn't be,
The whole shebang, kit and caboodle before me weary jellies:
Dying women raped in places they don't show on the telly,
Children beheaded for a quick kick around,
On invasion beaches the missionaries found,
Or little girls covered in sticky black flame,
For being born in the wrong place with different names.
These are the armies of the dead still rising from the dragon's teeth,
With the living still killing for a bit of golden fucking fleece.
You think she'd be proud when I exchanged sweet melody
Of pastoral hue for a note and a tone of misery's blue,
But opening her vein in a noble kind of way
She kissed this tainted orb a dramatic farewell –
So there I was like Paul McCartney down in the pit of hell;
Just when I dragged her up with a load of sugary wank,
I had a vision of a Chinese girl in front of a big bastard tank,
And I hit a note of such genius and dissonance
That my beloved's puckered lips burst and shrivelled in flame;

So now you find me 'ere drunk as a skunk,
Blabbering and jabbering about the price of fame.

M

Corporation Road's widened thoroughfare
Has sprouted space age lights
Sharply smartened up for the hordes of Saturday shoppers:
January is the cruellest month mixing bad credit with desire,
Poor families balance necessity with desperation to consume.
The half price shiny shoes, boots and leather jackets
Stand enticingly like girls of Amsterdam in their red-lit windows,
The broad grey pavement with its cold blue iridescence
Invites the townsfolk to pay tribute to the mighty Kubla Khan.
He's abandoned Xanadu for the quick fix of bacon double cheese,
In the dayglo colours of a palace roofed with M for mastery.
He is surrounded by his new breed of false grinned lackeys,
As his fighting six pack turns to ketchup-tainted lard
The sons and daughters of shipbuilders and steelworkers,
Put in endless shifts to multi wrap his greasy wares,
Salt the cardboard weapons of his all-embracing empire,
The same kind of Clearasil scented serfdom stretches
Over continents: Middlesbrough, Lyon, Bethlehem P.A.,
Bessemer furnace exchanged for deep fat frier,
Foundry sweat for stench of melted plastic cheese,
In Kubla's many M topped tributaries,
Where everything's available in extra large portions –
Except a higher purpose than the need to devour.

Job Satisfaction

"in religion the spontaneity of the human brain and heart acts independently of the individual as an alien, divine or devilish activity. Similarly the activity of the worker is not then his own spontaneous activity. It is the loss of his own self" Karl Marx

(i)

January and the cold slog to the factory
Seems much longer than it did before.

When the eight pints on a Friday night
Seemed glorious before a good hard fight,

When the chance of a fuck
Was foremost in my mind.

Now last night's beer turns my clogged mouth sour
As the six o clock bell begins the daily grind.

(ii)

A workday is a whirlpool
Of mind dulling daydreams-

The blunt ear battering piston-driven
MONSTER in the centre of the workshop
Drives your brain into a bloody mush.
Until all that remains is your hunger,
Your sex drive and a desperate humour
....well we all need a laugh!

(iii)

Well, let there be earthquakes
A sun black as sackcloth,

Let all eyes be smelted
As the stars crash down.

Let a blood-full moon
Tear apart sprawling great cities,

Let their gods take the lid
Off a world that's been twisted,

Let the beast cram his jaws
Skinfull of the worms….

(iv)

Sometimes at my lathe,
I suppress a shudder

At the dark things,
Shifting and growing inside me.

Well it just isn't on -
For a grown man to squirm.

To Look for America

The wise-cracking punk bus boy,
called him Frank Steamtrain:
"More tracks on his arms than Grand Central."
He had a manic stare and macho tash,
Vietnam vet but didn't speak of that,
He urged me to work hard sweeping floors,
The deadend motel for Frank was America.
My broom was the way to the top.
He told me as my mentor "Stop goofing off!
It's okay to smoke doob but first finish work.
Me I'm fucking the car park attendant,
I fixed her fridge then got into her icebox!"
It was understood I'd never repeat it,
Wife and kids Frank, the family man,
Entrusted me with his venereal secrets.
One night I was drunk and crazy door-kicking,
He picked me up in his Buick with one-eyed Tony
I told them it was love and I needed to see her,
"see Tony" said Frank " he understands all about yer,
He jumped off the town bridge to impress a woman
Lost his left eye on a rusty old bike frame",
"Listen man" said Tony " I like the cut of yer,
Take a swig on this bourbon and we'll go for a ride,
This is America where freedom is a good place to hide."

Tough

I can take a lot
You better believe it,
I can take it that it got to the point
Where you extracted the usual promises
Neither of us knew for sure could be kept.
Yeah, I can take that,
I'm cool playing the fool for you,
To lift your spirits – honey,
It's no skin off my nose.
I can take your appropriation
Of my favourite walks and places,
So that now our whirling ghosts
Dance there before my nauseous eyes,
They'll fade and there are other places
Where my soul can breath.
I can even take the way the words flowed –
Boiling clouds became picture poems,
Along with sudden blue jays,
Childhood forests,
Springtime chestnut candles:
I meant the words and they still
Have some light left in them.

But I can't take the morning
I picked up one of your shoes,
At the end of the crumpled love-made bed
While you sang and boiled our coffee,
The way I noticed for the first time
How tiny were your feet,
As I held the leather
In my hand like an injured bird,

Then placed it down
With the care of a surgeon.
Like Jimmy Cagney in Public Enemy,
It's down in the roots of me
And I'm forced to say
Enough,
I ain't so tough!

No, not so tough.

January Exile Haiku

Sex shop entreaties
Cold Soho bitter coffee,
Masochism rains.

—

Frosty businessmen
Flee to sleazy paid relief,
Grey river flows fast.

—

Phone card poetry:
"Spanking slave sucks good",
Lust boiled down hard.

—

Days without love,
Should I lick boots of leather?
Dry desolate nights.

—

Poetic silence
Library assistant's po-face,
Unreturned smile sticks.

—

Bear-baiting vision,
Exit pursued by Shakespeare,
Cruel love dog bites deep.

—

Dancing ghosts rise up
Half-baked salsa memory,
River swallows lovers.

–

Paving stones crooked edges
Play metal ceg boot beats,
Your ghost mouth opens.

–

Lone movie watching
Cinema crowd breathing soft,
Alone in a forest.

James Paints His Room

In his own fashion which means paying us
To do the job to his exact instruction.
At four pounds an hour it's my best job.
Compared to the burger-flipping bow-tied flunky
Bullshit I've subjected myself to,
It's downright dignified. Though Kelly and I
No doubt evoke the Laurel and Hardy theme
As James nods off after his afternoon Pils.
We sing brown-eyed girl but cannot wake him
With our merriness as we paint each wall
An entirely different colour so the world
Will never become fixed in the bedroom,
Where he now only needs to roll over
For a complete change of scene:
If it wasn't for the bubble gum pink radiator
I could almost wish to be a schizophrenic millionaire.

On James's Ceiling

Wild Prehistoric cave
painting horses run
From the brush
Of his Amazonian
Artist friend.
They gallop with abandon
through pure
White space
No dolloped artex here
To suck you in
When sweetly stoned;
They run out through the walls
Manes wind blown,
Too free to be held in:
We didn't do this at home.

James Stocks His Fridge with the Finest Veal

To piss off his vegetarian friends
In a calculated statement of political incorrectness,
Which fails to move me at two in the morning
In the middle of a three day session
Dedicated to skating on the surface of nothing
With the aid of bourbon and beer chasers.
As I slap chunks of the poor milk fed calves
Into the pan and horrify his aesthetic sensibilities
By chucking it into bread with brown sauce
In a calculated statement of class war,
That will be left out of his recounting,
When he is next entertaining his bourgeois friends
With the tribulations of his patronage
And the plebian poet kipping in his attic.

Ten Four in the Morning Ways for James to Die

Sausagebacondoubleeggmushroombeans
Teatwosugarstwoslicesdeeplyfried -
Every morning all that changes
Is the season and the difference
Between electric and natural light;
For a bit of variety he sometimes eats
Tomatoes instead of the beans.
(He prefers the squashy tinned variety.)

He cleans the ashtray
Once a week. Usually
On Fridays when it
Looks like Vesuvius
Before Pompeii – it's ready
To go, like the sound
Of the phlegm rattling
In his blackened lungs,
In the early dawn bathroom.

Then there's the car,
With the Pils and his medication
There's no need to expand
upon that idea.

The apocalyptic option
Remains a distinct possibility
Given the latest news;
Sometimes it seems
More comfort than horror -
Everyone you've loved
To go with you –
That depends he says,
On whom you've loved.

Rabies on a weekend run
To France to stuff the boot
With crates of cheap beer,
Some discount Beaujolais
And some blood thick claret.

The quiet option –
Maybe the saddest of all:
A midnight cardiac,
A hearts stopping moment -
It flips over,
An exhausted fish
In the chest cavity.
That's it – no more blood
Beats, no loss, no lust,
No laughs, no dreams, no love.

Newspaper paranoia inspired:
Savage senseless mugging
(with additional brutality –
maybe a chopped off finger,
or a bitten off nose,
acid in the face,
or a shard of glinting glass
applied to the jugular)
They like those little details
In the newspaper trade –
An angle, a story, an "in"
Worse if you're a woman:
No matter your complexion
You inevitably expire as
"an attractive blonde".

BIGFLASH PUBBOMB MOMENT !

Scraped off the pavement
In various ill fitting pieces.
As a contribution
To somebody's political statement –
Usually idealists,
Labouring under the notion
That anyone can be "free".

Let's throw in a little
Bit of glorious fantasy now:
At the point of "the little death",
The big one comes along.
As he sweats over the woman
He's been waiting all his life for
Who can walk though a storm
Light his fire and make it happen
The darling of a thousand faded
Popsters' raucous dreams,
Fading from his own eyes
As he pops his cork.

As always he treasures his eye
For the pathetic absurd
So the finale of this Decalogue
Is not an axe - wielding arsonist fiend,
Nor a ten storey sexual suicide,
But a half empty tin of pink salmon,
With a sharp edged, rusted lid,
Next to the alluring four pack
Of cold, cheap, supermarket lager.

Mystery Train

This is the last moment I'm sure of it,
Before the universe rolls itself into a ball
Then explodes again flinging everyone's atoms
To the twilight zone, the outer limits and beyond.
The illusion of chronological time.

This Northern station is unique this minute,
With the sunrise sky blood red
Over the horizon of houses and cathedral,
The people fascinating in various poses of ennui,
Contemplating divorces, children, work and nothing.

One girl's shivering in a fish-tail parka,
Bet she used to be a glimmering mermaid
Before they hauled her gasping to a loveless shore;
She thinks tonight she will design her own tattoo,
Something with fire and an eye in it.

I'm going to haul myself away again to a colder land,
Where bears poach reindeers, shamans drum on mushrooms,
Santa Claus is older than Jesus and trips on reindeer piss,
Cloaked in thick green furs and a great black hat
Like Isambard Kingdom Brunel's.

The world silently shifts on its axis,
Apocalyptic moment fails to materialise,
The red skies are obfuscated by cloud -
Home is a trudge through railway streets of rain,
Past grimly haunted siding scrubland.

The Flesh of the Bear

(For Thurid)

The flesh of the bear is tough and quite chewy
Greasy and gamey with a distinct aftertaste…..

Flying in, they melted,
The ice from the wings at Helsinki.
They could not however,
Thaw the black lump
In the pit of the gut.
Even the three glasses
Of free single malt
At Heathrow
Didn't do the de-icing.
Nor the beat up copy
Of Kerouac's "Big Sur":
Heated nightmare visions
Of raging California surf
Just making the iceball grip tighter.
So, Jack's stuffed and crumpled in
My back pocket while I assuage
My check-in panic attack
With pints of cold Guiness,
Feeding the lump further
Until I am cold in the head.
My luggage is not overweight
How many kilos is my foreboding?

Airports have a lot of primary colours -
Oz bright when your lifepump's hammering,
And your breath is beginning to whistle,
A bad bag-piped tune along to the muzac
From the dutyfree cave of glimmering glass,

What's calling me to Finland in this no-fit-state
To see my old friend after fitful correspondence,
Over ten wandering years from city to city,
In various states of laborious disarray?

The winter wound of another love laid waste,
Propelled me, no doubt onto jet then frozen prop plane,
With ice scraped from the wings at Helsinki
As the snow swirled until we disappeared
Into the air like a farmhouse in a twister –
There is no place like home,
No place such as home as we ascend
Through my fear of flying and dreams of forever falling,
Into fathomless oceans devoid of words and resurrections,
The winter wound of icicle sharp shattered promises,
From a cold neat tongue that left it's shards deep inside,
Freezing the vital organs like a Californian cryogenic quack.
Making of my mouth an empty globe-
A silent movie matte-card close-up unreal "Oh!"
Behind the glibness of my showman's patter.

Once upon a time long ago in a Sheffield far away
I said, vodka sodden, I was a small black bear,
You told me that you were an old grey fish,
Far below the waves in the cold mud of the Baltic,
So I supposed somehow you'd know the secret
Of unfreezing the animal's tongue from the burning ice.

So it's Thunderbirds are go into Stockholm and Helsinki,
Then whiskey refuelled onto Turku tumbling towards
The dark hours of Good Friday in days of five below,
With old Kerouac crucifying himself in my pocket
With bottle after bottle of sweet cheap Frisco Tokay
And the too familiar hysteria of hungover guilty visions:

Jack's off the road twisted Catholic satori
Has become my journey's totem
and I am his companion,
Travelling with him again
to the brink of nothing.

Later in the Sauna with my new friend your husband
I feel an old ghost stirring – a springtime incarnation
Fuelled by Finlandia in raucous beer frenzy,
Declaring undying friendship in joie-de-vivre night-ramblings.
I suppress a shudder at this sudden self's spectre,
Try to suck that spirit back into my shell.
I decide then to sleep in your cellar -
I am a bear in the darkness half awake
From a long creeping hibernation,
Whimpering in mad whispers to the ghost of Ti Jean,
"Dig it Jack man I am the king of the Kalevala
In the Northern land of my bear god familiar!"

So in the restaurant I consume the flesh of my brother,
Dreaming myself into shaman while crows gather,
Outside the boundaries of our conversation,
Ragged and brawling,
Flapping down onto steel-hard river glaze.
I imagine them bigger, ravens of Odin,
Sent down to me from the god hanging tree.
I try not to look insane in front of your children,
Hear myself talking about vodka and blinies.

Then comes the cracking,
The electric heart thumping moment.
I see the new line,
The fissure in the Aura river:
You both tell me, watch now
Soon it will all go –

Surprising that the crows don't rise in panic,
These vagabond birds are all set for ice surfing
As the grim floes shatter and the grey river flexes
For it's big spring push out into archipelago waters.
Finland, Easter, End of the Century
Dumbstruck poet bellyful of brown bear and bear label "olut"
Watching crow chancers surf out to the Baltic:
An internal cracking, a creak, a trickle, a gathering,
That will be a tearstorm on the banks of the Thames,
A molten flow of bitter words in Shakespeare's alehouse.

Cleansed by the wet heat of sauna and unfrozen Aura waters,
The black canker of cancerous ice broken by the bear god
Amid the timeless blessing of friendship,
In a country of silver birch and green pines,
Red granite rocks and impossible skies,
Coming around from its dark winter stupor.

Still, though, in the cool bookstore coffeeshop
Jack stumbles noisily towards death,
On a last torrent of drunken epiphanic mumblings,
A final holy fool's vision of Christ on the cross.
I cannot stay in Turku Cathedral on Easter morning-
It's not absolution that's required rather the restoration
Of my roar in the face of a snow white nothing,
No state of grace but some sense of "SISU"
To face up to a reckoning.

....the flesh of the bear is tough and quite chewy,
Greasy and gamey with a distinct aftertaste.

Welcome To Camp Ragnarok

The mosquito in the room tormented us all night,
Growing in size with it's incessant whine -
Suddenly coming from the strangest angles,
Till it ruled like a dark god from the Kalevala.
Our Torch battery flickered in the dark cabin,
Then faded leaving us to the sly fangs of the creature
That night time imagination had transformed,
Like nuclear waste in a Nippon monster movie.
Your heart was pummelling my bare chest
Like a Ṣami shaman deerskin drummer,
As my matchstick-propped open eyes
tried to see through gloopy darkness -
Only three hours in island summertime,
But eternities of blood at Nosferatu's leisure,
Until we got up at first light to see the dawn
Conjure the almost still sea into motion.
Hungry Pike twitching the hushed reeds,
Low salt water bubbling with sub-aqua life:
You watch as I cast a line and spinner
Into the early morning electric blue,
Instantly hooking the Moby Dick of Pike,
Cursing like Ahab as the great Baltic monster
Bends the rod double, pulling me over,
Finally snapping the black aluminium,
Dragging itself free, leaving us open mouthed
As it's striped bulk breaks the surface,
Then down to the reedy bed to gloat.
The world serpent of Viking Ragnarok
Has metamorphosised into this tiger fish.
All afternoon I work on thumping rhythm poems,
Try to summon Thor's killing hammer

To nail the world drowning bastard,
But the itchy Mosquito bites torment us
Till we succumb to sauna and warm afterlove;
As we fall into sleep I sense a deep stirring -
He's got all the time in the world,
Down there.

The Icarus Variations

(i)

The Shadow of the Birdman

The flickering of asthmatic
Night-time shadows,
Cast in pools of moonlight
On the bedroom wall.
Lungs squeezing deliberately in and out
Through the pipes
Of my own feathered squeezebox,
With it's out of kilter calliope nightmare music
Moulding the dark fluid shapes
In an Expressionist monster movie carnival.
Long Nosferatu fingers poking and prodding
At my panicked stillness with its scattered flock
Of feared imaginings wheeling around the room –

Around my floor-sleeping mother
With her easy beating breath,
Dropped off from her vigil at the
Foot of the bed where she terror-checked
That my laboured fluting
Did not come to the sudden,
Silent stop she silently imagined.

Years before, the old Scots doctor
Diagnosed and prescribed the small white
Amphetamine pills that left me
Weak kneed and fevered, with mind full
Of leaping running figures,
From the old red books my grandmother

Gave me, with their tales of
Transformation from human
To Narcissus flower.
From ravished girl
To sweet voiced nightingale.
From imprisoned boy
To soaring birdman:

The flock of wild budgies
In my chest's organ pipes
Thrilled to the name of Icarus
Even when I knew
of the hot wing-melted plunge
From the sun's fierce glory,
From the restraining fatherly wisdom,
Into the cold blue brilliance
Of the indefatigable ocean,

Because at night then
The monstrous shadows
Spread out arms feathered
And waxed by the songs
Of my internal flock of
Fluttering multicolour -

The shadow of the birdman and
My lost-boy shadow
Joined in curtain cracked lamplight
And moonlight,

Taking flight into the wing beating
World of ancient words
And the strange rhythmic names
Of my new crafty heroes

Odysseus and Orpheus
And my poor familiar Icarus:
Ever rising ecstatic,
Heedless of the heat from the
Fevered sun.

(ii)

The Heart of the Sun

September Twelfth and it's not the rerun
Of exploding towers I take to bed with me
Unable to lock away before dreamtime:
It's one black and white photograph,
From the myriad, almost pornographic pulp
Piles of the several newspapers on my desk,
With the shadowy figure of the man
Plummeting down umpteen floors.
I cannot imagine the collective horror
We have all just witnessed but this man
I can imagine all too well as sleep
Begins to wrap itself around my brain;
Desperate leap brings a childhood shadow
Flapping towards me and the image.
Feather by feather I give him wings
From my dreams and memories of America.
I do not know who he was but now
For a midnight moment we are the birdman -
The fall arrested as time runs backward.
Flash of light into dark corners -
The journey in from New Jersey,
Light rippled river with its dreamer's statue,
The birdman thrills to the incessant
Rhythm that makes this city ever-happening.

The birdman read all those books of beating words,
Of subway soup, jazz and heartbreak.
All those books of hitching desolation angels
And howling visionaries stretched
Like a breaking guitar string over the fretwork
Of this city with it's great towers and swirling
Guggenheim and King Kong Empire state
And poet's bridge with lonely Whitman
Welcoming the dawn with open heart.
The birdman felt he had at least gotten close to the
Sky and out of his smalltown childhood blues
With hamburger jukebox joints and homecoming queen,
Yes! - he married the homecoming queen:
The wind ripples through his peacock feathers
And through her corsage at the high school prom.
No! - he lost her to his best buddy, hefty captain
Of the football team and filled notebooks with
Badly written aching verse of life's unfairness.
Flashback to New Jersey shore walking behind
The perfect couple surrounded by horseshoe crab shells
Trying not to imagine her slender arms around him.
Hey but it was the birdman got the decent job
High up in the twin towers where the money
Goes round and around and what he makes
Helps keep his second love and family
In holidays to the Great Lakes, to the Forests
He dreams of in Ansel Adams images,
Whilst counting the hours at his desk way up.
Also the dough helps send him once in a while
To the Blackjack tables and roulette wheels at Atlantic City –
He's no plasterboard saint, my soaring birdman,
He remembers the electric thrill
Of the silver ball hitting black eleven,
Croupier's sardonic smile as he picks up the chips;

Riding in the rickshaws on the boardwalk,
Making Mafia jokes doing bad Brando impressions,
Bellyful of brandy and champagne with buddies
Guffawing and the night breeze the same
As when the early sailors wandered ashore.
Next day Catholic guilt and I-will-make- it- up- to-the-kids
And never-again-lord nostalgia in an old church,
Where childhood Catholicism draws him
To drip candlewax on hungover trembling fingernails.
His fear of becoming a Saturday Dad,
Like many of his friends, grabbing his gut like an icy fist.
The thought of stolen moments with his little girl
At the zoo or in the park instead of the goodnight kiss,
And watching her sleep counting her breathing
For five minutes to make sure it wouldn't stop.
All that everyday sentimental stuff can make
As many feathers for my birdman as any philosophy
Or theology, which he likes to ignore in favour
Of a vague feeling of benevolent non-interference.
Except when strapped in for takeoff on a 747
When he believes white knuckled that the Lord
Has a destiny for him to fulfil;
Then is this it? And is that it? start mushrooming
Up from the wells of his upside-down stomach,
And the sun is down and on the ground,
The birdman is not soaring but falling
To meet his own growing shadow.
The feathers I have given him begin to scatter
In the rushing up-draught and as they are torn away
The black and white birdman becomes a falling stranger,
Who I hope believed like Icarus until the last moment that
He would soar and loop the loop over the big apple,
But his memories and imaginings are lost to me.

The birdman meets his shadow and
Tumbles through the eye of the clock
To the place where time has stopped,
Tumbles into the fallen heart of the sun.
At Ground Zero the birdman is denuded
Of the dreamtime feathers I have endowed him
with. Each of the shafts loaded
With my projected and imagined memories.
Now he's the enigma of a so-called ordinary life
In the black and white news photograph,
Before the clay of his being
Is broken and shattered and mixed
With the smouldering dust of his assassins,
The fanatical Faustians who have sold today
For an imagined tomorrow,
Who now lie with my Icarus,
In the place where all clocks have stopped.
What innocent blood do they see
Streaming in the firmament?
Their molten metal wings disintegrated
In the heart of their artificial sun
Along with plumage of unimaginable hue:
The burnt up memories of every human mind
Lost to the hubris of fundamental belief-
The memories of wind and light and rain,
Of the seasons turning leaves,
And Sunday morning clarity,
And hopes and fears for family,
Sweet moments stolen from the mouth of Moloch,
Inscribed with romantic love and filial love,
Paternal love, maternal love, unrequited love,
Well-matured love, first flush love and tainted love -
So many delicate plumes left to flutter
In the minds of those left behind.

For it's only love and not revenge
That can remake for a moment the
Phoenix wings of the birdman,
Send him soaring again
Towards the Sun.

(iii)

Heavy Metal Resurrection

Wheezing again in broken rhythms in the cold dawn,
The calliope music is back; more out of kilter than before,
As the waking dream kaleidoscope switches uncensored,
From image to image in obscene technicolour,
Of shattered bloody limbs and grinning sadist jailers,
Crawling out of the Hieronimus Bosch crack,
Of war mongers in scoundrel attendance,
Sympathetic false smiles of slick torturers
Helping the crown-pierced Christ back up,
Onto the old bits of rough rasping wood,
In the wink of a 2000 year second,
Whilst the birdman is summoned in transformed splendour,
By besuited fools from the vast fiery void.
See what follows him pilgrim and turn your face away.
Those who can count life's value in black viscous barrels,
Have called him in his last incarnation,
To the slopes of the new technology's Golgotha,
Where they swap kids' bodies for innocent heads,
In a game where winning is just an illusion,
Blinded by the infra-red glare from the eyes
Of the earth-pounding air-soaring birdman,
As he casts his shadow on the mountains and the earth,
Ripping legs and arms from small frightened children,
His sharp feathers gleaming amongst the scattered collateral.

Body parts of grandmothers, mothers and men of "wrong" theology,
Bred by poverty, greed and years of colonial injustice,
With liberty's hypocrites bankrolling deprivation,
Building up dictators to grease wheels of exploitation,
Selling them weapons to hold down their people,
Who we then bomb to the stone-age or freedom,
Preaching the worth of the global village.
Where the privileged few hide behind nuclear weapons,
Leaving the outcast to be recruited by preachers of violence,
Who build a furious God from stark lives of stone,
While our leaders make incarnate the abomination.

Metamorphosised Icarus,
Boy of long ago innocent hope,
Swoops screaming to the earth now,
hurling chunks of the sun,
Shouting "obey!" to beings made of stardust,
Howling "Love our dream or die in fire!",
As he plummets and rises higher and higher,
Oil and blood dripping indistinguished,
So hard to breath when you see him;
Feathers of metal in the lungs of the poets,
Soon it will be the heart of the sun
He hurls at us
On his final plunge -
This once glorious boy resurrected in steel,
Whose sin it was to soar with pride.

Prelude to The Twocca Crow King

The Finn poets are being shown our special places,
My turn, so we climb the escarpment of Eston Hills.
Emerging from graffitied concrete underpass,
Walking over obscene messages on the painted path,
Treading over typical Teesside handles ending in "a" and "o",
JONNO DALLA ROBBO MACCA NOBBO
As the visitors smell bootchurned mud and teenage piss
I wonder how this compares to the scent of pine and birch,
Of rain in wild grass round lakes of teeming fish?
Start to point out English beech, sycamore and elder,
Beyond the spray painted remnants of the iron mines,
That welcome our breathless vision and notebook minds.
All overgrown with vandalism and dark green moss,
At the top of the steep abandoned railways incline.
Val tells Kalle of the rumour "Robin Hood woz 'ere"
While I roam off the path of the old railroad's course
To find a full-blown scarlet-topped Fly Agaric,
Glistening cap, spot-full of witch visions,
Shining in grey Autumn light beneath a gnarly oak.
So we speak of magic, legends and chewed human bones,
Then the years of furnace fire and multi-coloured smoke.
The Blade runner vista of what was I.C.I. captures our eyes,
As the chat shifts to industrial childhoods gone by,
When the sky burned red and metal clanged in the shipyard,
When the yellow river choked life out of foolhardy salmon,
And sulphur smells breeze-borne made Mams take in the sheets.
Even then this place was become haunted landscape:
Rails ripped up and old buildings pulled down or rotten,
Its men of iron fading ghosts of the working forgotten,
Barnaby Moor's pit top village nothing but a few bricks,
Swept by wind and rain and Northern snow into a whisper

Of a story I offer in semi-historical folk tale fragments,
For inspiration in the ears of our visiting friends.
How 'Blue Billy' gave his short sharp shocks,
In tall shafts where the dark spat rocks,
In this hollowed hill's cavernous whale belly,
Hundreds died to drag out ore for the world's need,
To be smelted into a serpent of shining steel,
That encircles the globe like the Ragnarok beast,
Spanning vast rivers, spawning rail tracks and weapons,
For the conquest of nations and imperial wars,
For defence of this island, from this small mountains core,
Before it was emptied and forgotten in the seats of power,
Till its secrets are in the keeping of the determined few.
Tales of past manglings and working class pride,
Come tumbling easy in a molten craic-flow from my lips.
Esa listens, drinking his DT-stopping Scotch in careful sips.
As we trudge and stumble up crude wooden steps to Nab Top,
The other times that were really mine come hurting into mind,
Young candied lips hot and soft in fresh summer,
Empty sketch pads and new prized horsehair brushes,
Virginal tubes of the most brilliant oils,
Opened up here for the very first time,
After painting tumbling in the vegetation and clover,
Bob Marley booming on the little black beat box,
"And is this love and is this love that I'm feeling?"
Then the half empty aftermath of fear for the future,
And the first cold kiss of mortality's intimations.
After that first splendour in our hill's wild grass,
While the other kids were revising for maths,
The moment hung and dangled on a piercing briar thorn,
Bees danced around us as the adult world was born.
We picked sweet bilberries and let them fall into tubs,
Thirstily eating as many with Keats-stained mouths,

Purple blotting out the desperation of dole days below,
Post-industrial kids who could only break out alone,
Mouthing the fine impossibilities of love and forever.
I slapped the greasy paint on with a palette knife;
Jam thick and inarticulate,
Chewed on the unspoken,
That would send me sprawling around the world,
Seeking the vision that always hangs just out of reach,
Appearing ephemerally in moments of waking dreams.
Now to be back here in Autumn with these other sight-seekers!
Speaking of old ghosts that still walk this route,
While the private spirits of our younger selves,
Still roam and ramble up here in our own Wuthering Heights.
You know, sometimes I thought I caught a sudden glimpse,
Beyond overgrown ferns, of our familiar figures.
When I've returned here with our miraculous daughter,
To find the fruit fields of our long ago innocence,
In timeless moments when her small soft hands,
Fill the bowl as we did with the little sweet globes,
That will fill Nana's fridges with abundance of Pie,
Those young incarnations flicker before my sun squinted eyes.
"Last year", I hear myself telling Henka and Jenni,
"the wild boys got stupid with lighter fuel and Swan Vesta's,
Burnt a wasteland in the bilberry patches and heather,
Prehistoric bracken ash-sprouted rapid over our heads,
And so we played explorers in a world of Dad and daughter"
I don't mention the mythical Eston Hills Crocodile.
Now there's a sense of frontiers and epiphanies lurking,
As Esa the electric shaman makes a manly Sisu sprint to the top,
A memory of the Crow totem hatches from deep within.
From the times I came here alone, cluttered and desperate,
In winter days of abandoned ways and lovers,
I tell Kalle that I always see him in dark times,

On a rocky outcrop by the old Martello Tower's ruins,
At the perimeter of the site of the iron-age fort,
Every time I've come here in a dolorous hour,
Read his presence as a challenge to myself to survive.
Know he's more than your average carrion devourer,
With his black wings stark against the frost and snow.
Suddenly the shiver down my bristling neck,
As we reach the sacred spot and see a haunch squatted man,
Face obscured by black cap and black hood,
At the edge of my personal legend's grey rock.
I nervously joke about him being The Twocca Crow King.
The dark keeper of the secrets of these hills,
Harbinger of death and saint of outlaw survival,
Later, I know, he will come to me and sing.